Fact Finders®

Biographies

Mary McLeod Bethune

Empowering Educator

by Lissa Jones Johnston

Consultant:
Kenneth Goings, PhD, Professor and Chair
Department of African American and African Studies
The Ohio State University
Columbus, Ohio

Capstone
press®

Mankato, Minnesota

Fact Finders is published by Capstone Press,
151 Good Counsel Drive, P.O. Box 669, Mankato, Minnesota 56002.
www.capstonepress.com

Library of Congress Cataloging-in-Publication Data
Johnston, Lissa Jones.
  Mary McLeod Bethune : empowering educator / by Lissa Jones Johnston.
  p. cm.—(Fact finders. Biographies)
  Includes bibliographical references and index.
  ISBN-13: 978-0-7368-6421-3 (hardcover)
  ISBN-10: 0-7368-6421-0 (hardcover)
  1. Bethune, Mary McLeod, 1875–1955—Juvenile literature. 2. African
American women educators—Biography—Juvenile literature. 3. African
American women social reformers—Biography—Juvenile literature. 4.
Teachers—United States—Biography—Juvenile literature. I. Title. II.
Series.
E185.97.B34J64 2007
370.92—dc22   2005037563

Summary: An introduction to the life of Mary McLeod Bethune, the African
    American educator who founded Bethune-Cookman College and the
    National Council of Negro Women.

Editorial Credits
John Bliss and Jennifer Murtoff (Navta Associates), editors; Juliette Peters, set designer;
    Lisa Zucker (Navta Associates), book designer; Wanda Winch, photo researcher/
    photo editor

Photo Credits
CORBIS/Bettmann, 9, 23; Florida State Archives, cover, 1, 7, 10, 13, 14, 15, 16, 17, 19,
27; Getty Images Inc./Kean Collection, 8; Getty Images Inc./Lightfoot, 5; Indianapolis
Recorder Collection, Indiana Historical Society, 21; Library of Congress, 25, 26

1 2 3 4 5 6   11 10 09 08 07 06

Table of Contents

Chapter 1

Eager to Learn

The McLeod family of Mayesville, South Carolina, worked hard on their small farm. Patsy and Samuel McLeod and their children spent their days picking cotton and tending the garden. The children did not attend school. There was no school in Mayesville for African American children to attend—until the day Miss Emma Wilson came to visit in 1886.

Wilson was a teacher at the new school for African Americans in Mayesville. She was walking from farm to farm, looking for students. She stopped at the McLeod farm and asked if any of the children would be able to attend school.

In the late 1800s, African American children often had to work in the cotton fields with their parents.

Patsy McLeod thought of her daughter Mary. Mrs. McLeod had always felt Mary was special. She knew Mary was eager to learn.

The McLeods could not send all of their children to school. But they knew this was a chance for Mary to achieve her dream. They quickly made their decision. Mary was going to school.

Chapter 2

Childhood

Mary Jane McLeod Bethune was born with her eyes wide open. Her mother said it was a sign that her daughter would do great things in her life. The date was July 10, 1875.

Bethune's parents were former slaves. They wanted their 17 children to be glad they were now free.

After the U.S. Civil War (1861–1865), the McLeods saved enough money to buy some land in Mayesville. They all worked on the family farm. Mrs. McLeod did housekeeping for her former owners. Mr. McLeod was a farmer and carpenter. Their children did many chores around the farm.

Samuel and Patsy McLeod
worked hard for their family.

Reading

Bethune played with some white children in the area. One day she picked up one of her friend's books. Her friend told her to put it down because Bethune couldn't read.

Bethune's feelings were hurt. She wondered why her white friend was taught to read, but she wasn't. Bethune made up her mind that one day she would learn to read.

In the late 1800s, many children learned to read using a horn book. A horn book is a single page, mounted on a wooden paddle, protected by a sheet of see-through cow horn.

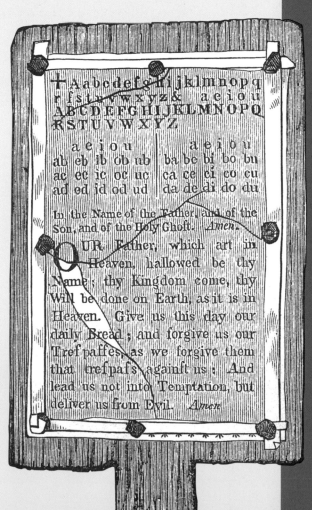

▲ Wilson's school for African American children was probably similar to this one.

School

Bethune grew up in a time when white people and African Americans had to live by different rules and laws. African American children could not attend white schools. Until Emma Wilson opened her school, the African American children of Mayesville had no school to attend.

Soon Bethune learned to read and write. Sometimes children who didn't go to school came to her house on Sunday afternoons. Mrs. McLeod encouraged her daughter to teach other children what she had learned.

Bethune grew up in this log cabin. The women in front are two of her sisters. ▼

More Studies

After about four years at Wilson's school, Bethune returned to work on her family's farm. One day, Wilson came to visit. A woman had given some money for one student to continue his or her education. Wilson decided Bethune would get the money.

Bethune went to Scotia Seminary in North Carolina. There African American women learned to be teachers and social workers. After graduation, Bethune attended the Moody Bible Institute in Chicago, Illinois. Bethune wanted to share her religious knowledge in other countries as a **missionary**. She was not allowed to be a missionary because she was African American. Bethune was disappointed.

Chapter 3

Teaching

Bethune returned home in 1895 and taught at Wilson's school for a few months. She learned how to run a school and how to raise money to keep it going. Soon she was ready for more responsibility.

Later that year, Bethune started teaching at Haines Institute in Augusta, Georgia. It was run by a woman named Lucy Laney. Laney taught Bethune that teaching was similar to missionary work. People in her own country needed Bethune's help.

Bethune left the Haines Institute and moved to Sumter, South Carolina, to teach at the Kendall Institute. In 1898, she married Albertus Bethune.

▲ Bethune, at far left, gained experience at Wilson's school, the Haines Institute, the Kendall Institute, and the Palatka Mission School that helped her start her own school.

The Bethunes moved to Savannah, Georgia, where Albertus had gotten a new job. In 1899, their son, Albert, was born.

Six months after their son was born, the Bethunes moved to Palatka, Florida. Bethune taught at the Palatka Mission School for four years until a new opportunity to use her skills came.

Bethune, in the dark dress, taught her students to prepare meals. ▼

Daytona Institute

One day a friend told Bethune that a school was needed in Daytona Beach, Florida. Many African American families lived there. Few schools existed for them. In 1904, Bethune moved to Daytona Beach. She rented a small house to be her school.

Daytona Institute began as a school for girls. Tuition was 50 cents a week. The girls studied reading, writing, and math. They also learned skills such as cooking, cleaning, and sewing. These skills helped students find jobs after graduation.

▲ At first, the Daytona Institute was only for girls. They learned reading, writing, and math, as well as skills that would help them get jobs.

Bethune worked hard to make her school a success. She sometimes had to fight for what she thought was right. Bethune did not believe in **segregation**. When white people attended programs at her school, she never separated them from the African Americans. Everyone sat together.

Bethune, in the dark robe, was proud of all her graduates. ▼

Bethune had little money to run her school. She and her students went to the city dump to look for old dishes, pans, and chairs to use. They used pieces of **charred** wood as pencils. She and her students sold pies and ice cream to buy supplies.

The Institute Grows

Bethune asked people in the community of Daytona Beach to support her school. She wrote articles, rang doorbells, and talked to people in community organizations. She never got discouraged when people said no.

But many whites and African Americans were happy to help. They gave money and donated services, such as carpentry and medical care.

After two years, Daytona Institute had 250 students. In 1923, it joined with another school and was renamed Bethune-Cookman College. Bethune was president of the school for almost 40 years.

Daytona Institute became Bethune-Cookman College in 1923. ▼

Chapter 4

Head, Hands, and Heart

Word spread about the success of Bethune's school. People admired her method of educating the "head, hands, and heart." Bethune trained her students to think with their heads. She taught them skills to do with their hands. And she encouraged them to serve and teach others from their hearts.

The NACW

In 1912, Bethune was invited to speak about her work at a meeting of the National Association of Colored Women (NACW). The NACW was a group founded to help poor African Americans.

Students at Bethune-Cookman College learned according to Bethune's motto of "heads, hands, and heart."

QUOTE

"Invest in the human soul. Who knows, it might be a diamond in the rough."
—Mary McLeod Bethune

The group raised money for child care, education, and housing needs. Bethune was honored to speak to these women. They shared her interest in helping others.

In 1924, Bethune became president of the NACW. As president of Bethune-Cookman College, Bethune focused on issues that affected her students and her school. In the NACW, she became interested in issues that affected African American families across the nation.

The NCNW

In 1935, Bethune founded the National Council of Negro Women (NCNW). The main purpose of the group was to make **politicians** in Washington, D.C., aware of issues affecting African Americans.

▲ As president of the NCNW, Bethune was a role model for young African American women.

Bethune wanted more African American women to become active in politics. She wanted them to hold leadership jobs in government. Bethune set up the NCNW to train African American women to achieve these goals.

Chapter 5

Working for the President

Bethune became known for her knowledge of African American issues. In 1936, President Franklin Delano Roosevelt appointed her to a job in the National Youth Administration (NYA). This was the first time a government job had been created for an African American woman. Bethune was the highest-ranking African American in the U.S. government.

The NYA was set up to provide training and jobs for young men and women. Bethune's work helped thousands of young African American people get valuable training for jobs.

In Washington, D.C., Bethune
worked with first lady Eleanor
Roosevelt. Aubrey Williams,
the head of the NYA, is on the right.

Bethune helped President Roosevelt
understand how important the NYA
was for African Americans. President
Roosevelt valued Bethune's opinions. He
often asked her how African American
people felt about other important issues.

Chapter 6

Building a Better World

Bethune was deeply saddened by the death of President Roosevelt in 1945. But she continued to work for important causes. In that same year, she attended the meeting that established the United Nations. Bethune met with people from all over the world. They discussed the importance of education and equal rights for all.

During her final years, Bethune retired from her duties at the NYA, the NCNW, and Bethune-Cookman College. She continued working for equal rights for African Americans and for women.

WHITE HALL

Students wish Bethune well after her resignation from Bethune-Cookman College.

QUOTE

"Look at me. I am black. I am beautiful."
—Mary McLeod Bethune

As Bethune grew older, she began to have health problems. On May 18, 1955, Bethune had a heart attack and died at her home in Daytona Beach. She was 80 years old.

Bethune poses in her office at Bethune-Cookman College.

The Dream Lives On

Throughout her life, Bethune used her education to help others and to be involved in her community. Bethune-Cookman College students are still encouraged to serve their communities. Bethune's organization, the NCNW, continues to help African American women be politically active.

As an educator, Bethune worked to end segregation and **discrimination.** The organizations she founded continue her dream of building a better world.

Fast Facts

Full name: Mary Jane McLeod Bethune

Birth: July 10, 1875

Death: May 18, 1955

Parents: Samuel and Patsy McLeod

Siblings: 16 brothers and sisters

Hometown: Mayesville, South Carolina

Husband: Albertus Bethune

Child: Albert McLeod Bethune

Achievements:

Springarn Medal from NAACP, 1935

Frances Drexel Award for Distinguished Service, 1937

Thomas Jefferson Award for outstanding leadership, 1942

Time Line

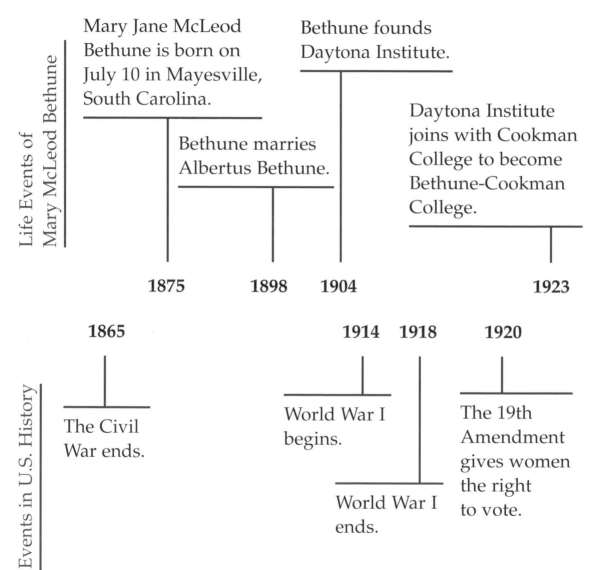

Life Events of Mary McLeod Bethune

Mary Jane McLeod Bethune is born on July 10 in Mayesville, South Carolina.

Bethune founds Daytona Institute.

Daytona Institute joins with Cookman College to become Bethune-Cookman College.

Bethune marries Albertus Bethune.

1875 1898 1904 1923

1865 1914 1918 1920

Events in U.S. History

The Civil War ends.

World War I begins.

World War I ends.

The 19th Amendment gives women the right to vote.

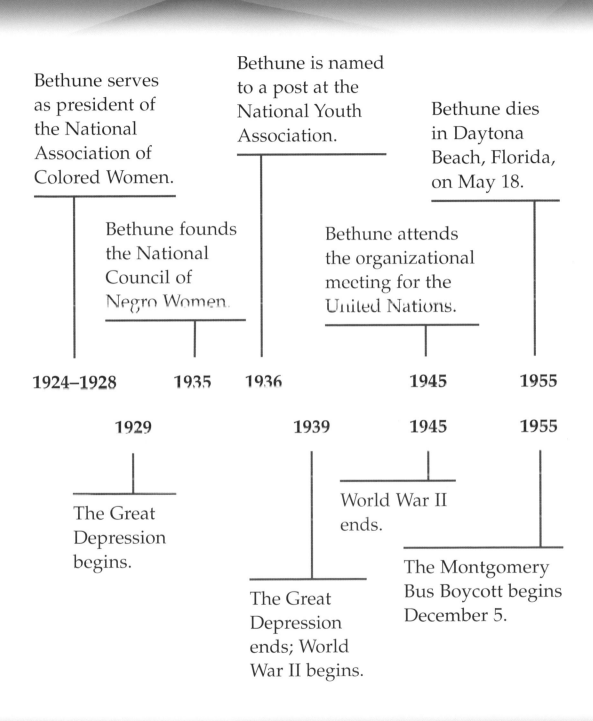

Bethune serves as president of the National Association of Colored Women.

Bethune is named to a post at the National Youth Association.

Bethune dies in Daytona Beach, Florida, on May 18.

Bethune founds the National Council of Negro Women.

Bethune attends the organizational meeting for the United Nations.

1924–1928   1935   1936   1945   1955

1929   1939   1945   1955

The Great Depression begins.

World War II ends.

The Great Depression ends; World War II begins.

The Montgomery Bus Boycott begins December 5.

Glossary

charred (CHARD)—burned slightly or partly

discrimination (diss-krim-i-NAY-shuhn)—unfair treatment of people based on age, race, gender, or other differences

missionary (MISH-uh-ner-ee)—someone who is sent by a church or religious group to teach that group's faith and do good works, especially in a foreign country

politician (pol-uh-TISH-uhn)—someone who runs for or holds a government office

segregation (seg-ruh-GAY-shuhn)—the act or practice of keeping people or groups apart

Internet Sites

FactHound offers a safe, fun way to find Internet sites related to this book. All of the sites on FactHound have been researched by our staff.

Here's how:

1. Visit *www.facthound.com*

2. Choose your grade level.

3. Type in this book ID **0736864210** for age-appropriate sites. You may also browse subjects by clicking on letters, or by clicking on pictures and words.

4. Click on the **Fetch It** button.

FactHound will fetch the best sites for you!

Read More

Evento, Susan. *Mary McLeod Bethune.* Rookie Biographies. New York: Children's Press, 2004.

McKissack, Patricia, and Fredrick McKissack. *Mary McLeod Bethune: A Great Teacher.* Great African Americans. Berkeley Heights, N.J.: Enslow Publishers, 2001.

Somervill, Barbara A. *Mary McLeod Bethune: African-American Educator.* Our People. Chanhassen, Minn.: Child's World, 2004.

Index